# MARBLES
## A PLAYER'S GUIDE

**Shar Levine
& Vicki Scudamore**

illustrated by Emily S. Edliq

**Sterling Publishing Co., Inc.**
New York

*In loving memory of my mother, Dorothy Levine. To Elaine Humphrey and her son, James Humphrey, who always come to my rescue. Thank you for your friendship, support and computer wizardry. As always, to Paul, Shira, and Josh; I guess I haven't lost my marbles after all these years with you.—S. L.*

*To my mother, Florence Lorber-Parecki, who with her loving patience taught me to play fair, and to my sister, Katie Lorber-Christie, and brother, Harold Lorber, who played with me anyway! Thanks to my wonderful husband, Charles, who has always supported me in whatever I do, and to my sons, Brian and Trevor, and daughter-in-law Lisa.—V. S.*

*To Jason, for always being my best friend and sunshine, and for inspiring me in every element of life. To my family, who have continually loved, supported, and encouraged me in all my endeavors. And to Ashley Jordan—the sweetest little addition to my life.—E. E.*

**Acknowledgments**
The authors would like to thank Larry Van Dyke of the Sea-Tac Marbles Club for his time and expertise. We are grateful for the use of his marble collection and his support for our book. We are indebted to Leslie Johnstone for her assistance and photographic talent. Our thanks to Marsha Assouline for her ideas on marbles and pottery. Thanks also to Alan Romano, of House of Marbles, Teign Valley Glass, for his advice.

We would particularly like to acknowledge and thank the Robert Held Art Glass Studio, Vancouver, B.C., Canada, and its talented glassblowers, Robert Gary Parkes and Michael Kuhlmey, for their generosity and kindness. Michael took time off from his busy day to create special marbles, which are featured in this book. Trevor Scudamore drew the marble bag on this page. And last, but not least, to Bob Block; you're great!

Designed by Wanda Kossak; edited by Isabel Stein. Photographs by Shar Levine, assisted by James Humphrey, and by Leslie Johnstone.

**Library of Congress Cataloging-in-Publication Data**

Levine, Shar, 1953-
    Marbles : a player's guide / Shar Levine & Vicki Scudamore ;
illustrated by Emily S. Edliq.
       p.    cm.
    Includes index.
    Summary: Provides information on the history of marbles, how
they are made, different kinds of marbles, and the games you can play
with them.
    ISBN 0-8069-4262-2
    1. Marbles (Game)—Juvenile literature.  2. Marbles (Game objects)—
Juvenile literature.  [1. Marbles (Game objects)  2. Marbles (Game)]
I. Scudamore, Vicki.  II. Edliq, Emily S., ill.  III. Title.
GV1213.L48  1998
796.2—dc21                    98-26083
                              CIP

10  9  8  7  6  5  4  3  2  1

First paperback edition published in 1999 by
Sterling Publishing Company, Inc.
387 Park Avenue South, New York, N.Y. 10016
© 1998 by Shar Levine & Vicki Scudamore
Distributed in Canada by Sterling Publishing
% Canadian Manda Group, One Atlantic Avenue, Suite 105
Toronto, Ontario, Canada M6K 3E7
Distributed in Great Britain and Europe by Chris Lloyd
463 Ashley Road, Parkstone, Poole, Dorset, BH14 0AX, England
Distributed in Australia by Capricorn Link (Australia) Pty Ltd.
P.O. Box 6651, Baulkham Hills, Business Centre, NSW 2153, Australia

*Printed in Hong Kong*

Sterling ISBN 0-8069-4262-2 Trade
              0-8069-6257-7 Paper

# Contents

## MARBLE BASICS

# GAMES

## MARBLE ARCADES

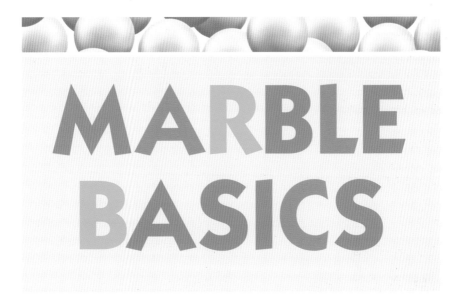

# MARBLE BASICS

# Introduction

Although you or your friends may just be discovering the fun and games associated with marbles, these beautiful glass spheres have been around for ages. Down through time, adults as well as children have played marble games.

The games have been passed down by word of mouth in most cases, and the origins of the names sometimes have been lost. Some games have names that pretty much explain themselves. Span refers to a handspan or the distance between your thumb and your pinkie (little finger) or third finger when your fingers are spread out. String of Beads looks just like a string of beads and Bombers—well, you get the idea.

Some games have names that make no sense at all today. Names vary from region to region, and even from playground to playground. This book uses common names found in schoolyards around North America. You and your friends may know the same game by another name. If you are searching for a game and you can't find it by title, look at the descriptions of the games to see which it is.

You may wish to create your own games. Write down the rules, so that everyone knows how to play. If the game is popular enough, it may soon spread to other kids in other cities!

# WARNING

Marbles are fun to play with and beautiful to look at, but they can also be deadly! No child under the age of 5 should be allowed to play with marbles.

Do not put marbles in your mouth. If you swallow a marble, it can block your air passage, and you will not be able to breathe.

If you have a younger brother or sister around the house, make sure you do not leave your marbles where he or she can find them. If you are playing indoors and you are playing for friendlies, count your marbles before you start playing. At the end of your games, count them again. Be sure you put away as many marbles as you started with.

Look under all the furniture to find stray marbles. Young children tend to see these shiny objects and place them in their mouths.

If for some reason a child should swallow a marble, tell an adult right away.

Don't place marbles in any other body openings, either. Do not shove marbles up your nose or push them into your ears. Each year emergency rooms all over the country see frantic parents accompanied by crying kids who have favorite marbles stuck in their noses. These marbles are painful to remove.

It may be really funny in movies to see people trip on marbles, but it is not so funny in real life. Don't leave marbles on the floor when you are finished playing. A person who trips and falls on them can break bones or get a nasty bump on the head.

Marbles can be harmful to pets. Dogs sometimes like to chew on marbles. If a dog crunches a glass marble, the broken glass can be really painful! The only pet who should have marbles is your fish. Marbles make excellent decorations at the bottom of aquariums.

# Guide to
## the Book

 Marble players can be called mibsters; marbles used for shooting are sometimes called taws, and target marbles are called mibs or kimmies. This can get pretty confusing. To make it simpler for the reader, this book will use easy-to-follow terms:

- The person whose turn it is is called *the player*.
- The person you are playing against is called *your opponent* or *the next player*.
- The marble you are shooting at is called the *target marble*.
- The marble you use to shoot at other marbles is called *your shooter* or *your taw*.

We have included setup diagrams, so you'll know how to place your marbles to start a game.

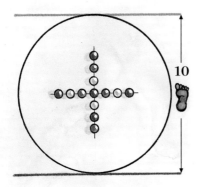

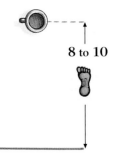

A spread hand shape on the diagram equals the distance of one handspan.

A foot shape with a number tells you the distance to measure in feet.

10 = 10 feet, for example.

Except for Ringer or if you're playing in a tournament, these distances don't have to be exact, so you can use your own hand or foot to measure in most cases.

The diagrams are color-coded as follows:

| COLOR | MEANING IN THIS BOOK |
|---|---|
| black marble | your shooter |
| red marble | the marbles you have put into the game |
| blue, yellow, and green marbles | your opponents' marbles, which they have put into the game |
| solid blue line | the lag line (if there is one) |
| orange line | the taw line (shooting line) |
| purple line | the pitch line (if there is one) |
| dashed blue line | measurement line for distances |

The backgrounds of the setup diagrams for the games are colored to show off the color of the marbles, but you can't tell the kind of surface by the color in the book. Suggested playing surfaces are given in the game's instructions.

# History of Marbles

 Imagine sitting on the banks of the Nile, watching the pyramids being built. To pass the time on the long, hot days, you and a buddy start playing a friendly game of marbles. It's hard to believe, but games of marbles have been around since ancient times. Glass marbles have only been around for about 600 years, but marbles of clay or stone, and even fruit pits, were used for rolling games long before that.

To give you an idea of just how long marbles have been around, follow the marble time line below:

**4000 B.C.**    Clay marbles placed in tombs of Egyptian pharaohs.

**3000 B.C.**    Marble-shaped objects placed in tombs in Eastern Ireland.

**2000–1700 B.C.**    Red-brown clay marbles made in Crete.

**420 B.C.** Greek vase shows goddess playing with knuckle-bones (anklebones of cloven-hoofed animals).

**100 B.C.** Clay marbles in pueblo dwellings in what is now southwestern United States and Mexico.

**10 A.D.** Castles or Pyramid played, using nuts, in Rome.

**200 A.D.** Soapstone spheres placed in Hopewell Indian mounds in what is now Ohio.

**300 A.D.** Romans played games with polished nuts or knucklebones and brought the game with them everywhere in the world they conquered and settled.

**900 A.D.** Glass marbles made in Venice, Italy.

**1300s** Marbles played with throughout the Middle Ages.

**Early 1500s** A game called *trou madame* described by French author Rabelais, in which small marbles were rolled into holes at one end of a board. When the game arrived in England it was called *trunks* or *troll-madame*.

**1560** Children are shown playing marble games in Pieter Brueghel the Elder's famous painting *Kinderspiele* (*Children's Games*).

**1600s** Shakespeare writes of a game called cherry pit, in which polished stones were tossed into holes in the ground. Water-powered grinding mills are used for the manufacture of locally mined marble and alabaster marbles in Germany.

**1720** Daniel Defoe, author of *Robinson Crusoe*, writes of a marble player "so dexterous an artist at shooting the little alabaster globe ... that he seldom missed."

**1800s** China factories in Germany begin specializing in making china marbles. Marbles of agate made in Germany, many for the American market. They became so popular that the word  "aggie" is used for all stone marbles, and sometimes for all playing marbles.

**1846** Marble scissors were invented by a German glass-blower, which sparked mass production of varied colors and intricate patterns.

**1840s** Clay marbles made in an Ohio factory at the rate of 100,000 a day. Called "commies" or "commoneys," they were the common everyday marbles.

**1902** M. F. Christenson patents a machine to make machine-made glass marbles in Akron, Ohio.

**1914** World War I stops the supply of marbles from Europe to North America. To meet the demand, marble production in the U.S. increases.

**1920s** Fully mechanized marble-making developed.

**1922** First national Ringer tournament in U.S. held in New Jersey.

**1925** Method of machine-feeding 3 colors for swirls developed.

**1940s** Many servicemen play marbles for fun during WW II.

**1950s** Japanese cat's eye marbles become popular.

**1970s to present** Most machine-made marbles made in Asia and Mexico.

# How Marbles Are Made

There are various ways of making marbles. Try this. Take a small piece of clay or dough. Roll it between your palms or on any flat surface. Can you make a completely round ball? The answer is most likely *no*. Imagine trying to manufacture millions of these shapes, all the same size and all perfectly round. This is the problem that marble manufacturers have had for centuries. Marbles are made in large batches by a few manufacturers around the world. You need special machines and materials to make marbles.

## Machine-Made Glass Marbles

Here's the basic idea of how machine-made marbles are made today:

1 Cullet, usable excess glass from a larger operation in the factory, is made from broken and discarded glass.

2 The cullet is melted in a glass furnace or tank at a very high temperature (more than 2400°F or 1315°C). Special oxides like cobalt oxide or iron oxide are added to the molten glass to give it color.

3 The melted glass is poured through a small opening, adjusted to the size of the marble desired. The stream of glass is then cut into equal-sized pieces by machine-operated shears.

4 The small cut pieces then travel down feeders to rollers. The rollers have a perfect half-round groove cut in a spiral along the whole length of each roller. As the molten glass travels down the grooved rollers that are turning at the correct speed for the glass to roll down to the end while still hot, the groove is perfectly matched to make a round marble. As the marble travels down the rollers, it cools.

5 At the end of the roller, the marbles are dumped into an annealer, a hot oven that slowly cools the glass marbles down to room temperature. This slow cooling relieves all the stress and strain that the glass had inside it while the marble was made. The marbles must be annealed (slowly cooled and hardened) or they will crack or break from the stress and strain inside.

6 Workers check the marbles created to be sure that they are identical in size and shape and have basically the same colors or designs.

## How Do They Get the Colors Inside a Marble?

Have you ever wondered how the colors got into glass marbles? Each color is the result of a mixture of different ingredients, in addition to the basic sand, soda ash, feldspar, and fluorspar that make glass. For example, some white marbles are colored with zinc oxide. Other coloring agents include cobalt oxide and black copper oxide. Some early pink marbles were colored by having a gold coin thrown into the molten glass in the tank. Recipes were developed over the years and were sometimes jealously guarded by manufacturers.

The varying ingredients cause the different colors of glass to have different densities, so the colors don't mix together when melted. Temperature and timing are also crucial for coloring. Over the centuries, people developed many ingenious ways of getting colors in the center of and on the surface of marbles, both handmade and machine-made.

## Handmade Glass Marbles

Before there were machine-made marbles, all marbles were handmade. The Robert Held Art Glass Studio, in Vancouver, B. C., is Canada's largest glassblowing facility. At the studio they still make handmade marbles using the same techniques marble makers have used for hundreds of years. Two of the glassblowers who work there, Michael Kuhlmey and Robert Gary Parkes, spend their lunch hours and weekends creating marbles which are beautiful works of art.

Collection of handmade marbles from Robert Held Art Glass Studios. A star cane was used to make the one with stars.

Here's how one kind of handmade marble is made:

1 Blobs of molten glass are gathered on a metal rod called a punty. Then the punty is rolled on a metal table called a "marver," where the glass is cooled and rolled into a cylinder. A paper pad is used to help give the molten glass shape.

2 While the glass is molten, the glassblower adds tiny bits of colored glass, powdered glass, or long straw-shaped colored glass canes. These will give the marbles their design or color. A large glass cane or rod is built up to the pattern, width, and color the glassblower wants.

3 The glassblower continuously rolls his punty on his bench, while he shapes and forms the marble. He must reheat the glass in a small, very hot furnace to continue to shape the glass.

Two sharpened canes and a twisted cane, used in handmade marbles.

**4** When the glass is pliable enough to mold, the glassblower cuts a rounded blob from the rod, using special shears. The final, almost perfect marble is shaped in a small metal tool called a block.

**5** The rounded, cut marble is then placed under a blowtorch to smooth and seal the glass.

**6** The hot marbles are then cooled overnight in an oven, so they will harden without becoming brittle. Each marble is unique and may be signed by the artist.

When the glassblower is creating a marble, the molten glass usually appears bright orange. The temperature of the glass is over 1800°F (1000°C). As the glass cools, it changes color. The first lesson a glassblower learns is never pick up a piece of glass that has fallen on the floor. Even though a piece of glass may look cool and solid, it keeps its heat for a long time. Glass must be cooled slowly, so that it doesn't crack or break.

The glass rod from which the marble will be cut is put in the furnace to keep it soft and easy to work.

Trimming the end of the glass rod.

A roughly shaped marble at the end of a clear glass rod on a punty.

## Visit a Marble Factory

If you are fortunate enough to live near a glass-blowing studio, ask your teacher to arrange a tour of the studio.

Shaping a marble in a mold or block.

# Marble Facts

## The Marble Stone

Certain statues and columns are made from a stone called marble, found in many places around the world. Marble comes in many colors, including white, grey, tan, and even pink. In earlier times, small pieces of marble stone were rounded and used in games. Some people think this is where the word *marble* comes from.

## Did You Know

There are marbles called end-of-day marbles. They are usually large and are one-of-a kind marbles. It's believed that glassblowers used bits of leftover glass at the end of the day to make these marbles to give to neighborhood children as gifts.

## Try This

Pour an ounce of honey in a glass and some clear syrup in another glass. Gather the honey on a swirled wooden honey paddle or honey spoon by dipping the spoon into the honey and turning the spoon until it is coated in a thin layer. Dip this coated spoon into the syrup and turn the spoon again, coating the honey layer with the syrup layer. This is what the glassblower does with the molten glass in order to create a handmade 2-color swirl marble.

# Marble Names

Here are some marble names and what they mean:

Antique aggie.

**Aggies:** Marbles made of a hard stone called agate. These marbles are much prized for their shooting quality. (Aggies can mean marbles in general, also.)

Antique alleys.

**Alleys or allies:** Get their name from alabaster, which is a soft stone related to marble, but alleys have come to mean very good marbles, or marbles in general.

Collection of Benningtons.

**Benningtons:** Got their name from Bennington Pottery, in Vermont, which made some spotted pottery that resembled these marbles. Benningtons are blue- or brown-glazed clay marbles that aren't completely round. A Bennington has a circular unglazed spot that results from its touching another marble while still wet with glaze.

**Bumboozer:** A large marble of agate or glass.

Bumboozers with a peewee.

**Cat's Eyes:** Clear marbles with different-colored blades or vanes inside. It is unusual to have black vanes inside this type of marble.

Cat's eyes of different sizes.

**Chinas:** Marbles made of china or porcelain clay, which uses white kaolin clay as a base. There are both glazed and unglazed chinas. (Glaze is a shiny glass coating.)

Unglazed chinas (at top). Glazed chinas (at bottom).

**Clearies:** Clear glass marbles made of a single color throughout; could be colorless, light blue, green, etc.

Clearies of various sizes.

**Clouds:** End-of-day marbles with colored flecks of glass that aren't stretched, which look like clouds floating over the core (the center part of the marble).

Clouds.

**Comics or Comic Strips:** Marbles with comic book characters on the surface. Only made for a brief time period, so they are rare.

Comics.

Old commies.

**Commoneys or Commies:** Originally meant common marbles made of clay; today means everyday or common glass marbles.

**Corkscrews:** Marbles with 2 or more colors in spiral designs. In corkscrews, the spirals rotate around the marble from one pole to the other, but don't meet.

Corkscrews.

Purees.

**Glassies or Puries:** Clear, brightly colored glass marbles.

**Immies:** Glass marbles streaked with color so they look as if they were made of real agate. "Immie" is short for "imitation."

Immies.

Milkies.

**Milkies:** Opaque, milky white marbles.

**Onion skins:** End-of-day marbles in which the colored flecks of glass are stretched so the core has many swirls, resembling an onion.

Onion skins.

Peewees with bumboozer.

**Peewees:** Small marbles, usually $1/2$ inch wide (1.2 cm) or less.

**Steelies:** Ball bearings used as marbles. Many ball bearings are used for industrial purposes. Metal marbles cannot be used in tournament play.

Steelies.

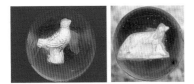

Sulfides.

**Sulfides:** Clear marbles which have clay figures inside. Many of these are very valuable marbles.

**Swirls:** Could be handmade or machine made. The handmade ones have bands or strands running from pontil mark to pontil mark.* The machine made ones have swirls of colors injected into the base stream of glass. *

Handmade swirls.

*The pontil mark is the mark left when a handmade marble is cut off the punty (iron rod) or off the molten glass cane.

# Marble-Playing Words

 If you're going to walk that walk, you have to talk that talk. To be a real marble player, you have to know the lingo. Here are some common marble terms and words. Some of the words vary from city to city, or even from schoolyard to schoolyard. See how close these words come to the ones you are using with your marble-playing friends.

**Bombing** or **Bombsies:** Dropping your marble onto another marble.

**Dubs:** When two or more marbles are knocked out of a ring with one shot. Also another name for Ringer.

**For Fair** or **Fairsies:** Rules of playing in which each player gets back his or her marbles at the end of the game. This is the best way to start playing, as you won't lose all your marbles while you are just learning the game.

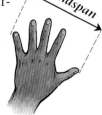

**Fudging:** Moving your hand forward while shooting, or in some other way cheating. This includes placing a hand over the ring or taw line during shooting or having your knuckles off the ground when they're supposed to be touching the ground. In tournament play you lose a shot for fudging.

*handspan*

**Handspan** or **Span:** How you measure a distance in marbles. Open your hand as wide as you can. The distance between the end of your thumb to the end of another finger, usually your pinkie (little finger) or third finger, is a span. Note: children who play musical instruments, particularly piano, have wide handspans.

**Histing:** Lifting your hand before shooting when your hand is supposed to remain on the ground.

**Hunching:** Another word for fudging. Moving your hand forward when shooting before the shooter has left your hand, or moving your hand over the edge of the ring in tournament play.

**Keepsies:** Rules that any marbles that a player loses aren't returned at the end of the game, but kept by whoever won them.

**Kimmies or Mibs:** The marbles you are aiming for in the game.

**Knuckles down** or **Knuckling down:** Shooting a marble with one or more knuckles touching the playing surface until the shooter leaves your hand. Required in some games.

**Lagging:** In marbles you don't flip a coin to see who goes first, you lag. Shoot or bowl a marble from the pitch line to another, parallel line (the lag line) drawn about 10 to 15 ft (3 to 4$^1$/$_2$ m) away from the first line. The player whose marble is closest to the lag line, on either side of it, goes first.

**Lag line:** The line you throw towards in lagging.

**Mibs:** Target marbles; the ones you're shooting at.

**Mibster:** A marble player.

**Pitch line:** The line you stand behind to lag.

**Plunking** or **Jumpsies** or **Skipping:** Shooting your marble in such a way that it jumps up into the air and hits the target marble on landing without hitting the ground first.

**Pot:** Collection of marbles that every player adds to for playing a game.

**Shooter:** The marble you shoot with. It may be slightly larger than a regular marble. Some players have favorite or lucky shooters. Also called a taw.

**Shooting line:** The line behind which you stand (or knuckle down) to shoot in many games. (Could be a circle.)

**Slip:** When a marble slips out of a player's hand accidentally.

**Snooger:** Term used in Ringer to describe a target marble that is near the rim of the ring. It can also mean a near miss or close call.

**Span:** The distance between the end of your thumb and any other stretched out finger, usually your pinkie or third finger.

**Target marble:** The one you are aiming at.

**Taw:** The marble you're shooting with; shooter.

**Taw line:** Shooting line. The line behind which you stand (or knuckle down) to shoot in many games.

# How to Shoot

Certain techniques of shooting work better than others. Three basic ones are given here.

## Knuckling Down

This is the time-honored method by which marbles are shot.

1 Put your knuckles on the ground and curl your fingers. If you are playing on a rough surface, you can rest your fingers on a piece of cloth. (Depending on the game, the rules may specify how many knuckles must be on the ground.)

2 Place a marble in the curve of your pointer finger. Hold the marble there with your thumb behind it.

3 Aim your marble by slightly adjusting the angle of your hand.

4 When you think you've got it, shoot the marble by pushing it out with your thumb. Don't lift your hand as you shoot or move it towards the line.

## Bowling or Rolling

This is an underhand throw, the same method you would use when rolling a ball for bowling. It is the easiest way of shooting for a small child who is just starting the game. You may use this method in most games (but not in Ringer).

● Hold the marble in your palm and roll the marble towards your target.

## Flicking

This method gives a marble a lot of speed, and when a marble shot in this manner comes in contact with its target, it can cause a big reaction.

1 Place the marble on the surface you're shooting from, and place the tip of your thumb down behind it.

2 Curl your pointer finger or middle finger to the first joint of your thumb and aim at your target.

3 "Flick" or straighten your pointer finger rapidly to connect with the marble and watch it fly!

## Spanning

This technique is used in some games, like Spangy. If you are allowed to span and a marble lands within a handspan of your target marble, open your hand wide. Place your thumb next to the shooter and another finger, usually your pinkie or third finger, next to the target marble. Close your hand in such a manner that the marbles knock together. If you can do this, both marbles belong to you. (If you miss, you may lose your shooter, depending on the game.)

## The Right Spin

What is backspin and why do you need to know? If you ever watch a game of tennis, you will see that players use different spins on their balls. Some spins will cause the ball to bounce off in a different direction, while other spins will cause the ball to drop and not bounce at all. You can give a marble backspin also.

Backspin is a rotary motion you give to your marble when you shoot so that it will stay in one place after it hits another marble. If you can use backspin, it will help you in certain games, like Ringer. As you are about the shoot your marble, place just a little pressure on it with your pointer finger. This will cause the marble to spin or rotate.

## The Right Marble

In marbles, bigger is not necessarily better. The smaller the marble, the easier it is to accurately aim and shoot. The larger marbles are better for games such as Dropsies or Bombers, or make great trading marbles, but they aren't the best shooting marbles.

Another myth is that a marble ought to be smooth and unblem-ished. According to marble champions, rough or pitted marbles are the best shooters. A marble with a tiny groove in which you can place your fingernail will give you the best backspin and fastest shot.

Marbles that are collector's items should never be used in play, and should be smooth and unmarked. A playing marble can have imperfections.

Immies.

## Size

Huge marbles are generally not used to shoot. In tournament games, marbles must be a certain size. In Ringer, a shooter must be between $1/2$ inch and $6/8$ inch (1.2 and 1.9 cm) in diameter, and the target marbles should be $5/8$ inch (1.6 cm) in diameter. Generally marbles fall into 4 categories when grouped by size: peewees (less than $1/2$ inch in diameter), average-sized marbles ($5/8$ inch in diameter), shooters ($1/2$ to $6/8$ inch), and bumboozers (very large marbles).

Marbles of different sizes from peewee (at right) to bumboozers (two at left).

## The Science of Marbles

Playing marbles is a basic introduction to physics, the science of forces and motion. When your shooter hits another marble, it causes it to move in a certain direction. The direction in which the hit marble moves depends on a number of things, including the spin of the marble as you shot it, the places on the marbles where they came in contact, and the playing surface. Combine any or all of these factors with the speed or force at which you shot the marble, and that's what makes the game interesting!

To better understand how marbles move, watch a game of pool or billiards. You will see how the billiard balls move in certain ways when they are hit. Good players can predict their shots using the laws of physics. Of course, it is easier to tell where a billiards or pool shot is going to go, because the surface of the table is completely smooth and flat and the balls are large enough to hit in exact spots. It is much harder to accurately hit a tiny marble on an uneven piece of concrete!

With a steady hand, good eyesight, and some basic understanding of physics, you can improve your chances of winning at marbles.

# Rules and Such

 If marbles is a game serious enough to play in tournaments, then there have to be some rules. Each marble game in this book has basic guidelines. You may adapt or change some of the rules to fit the situation, but any changes should be agreed upon by all players before you begin the game. Some rules which you will have to determine for yourself include:

1 What happens to the marbles when you have to stop the game for dinner or for the school bell?

2 What happens when the playing surface is disturbed? This usually occurs when your cat or dog decides to play his own game with your marbles.

3 Do younger children get any breaks on shooting?

## Lagging

Rather than flipping a coin or guessing a number, a process called lagging is the time-honored way of seeing who shoots first. The person who gets to go first in marbles has an advantage. If the player is skilled, he or she may hit and claim all the marbles before the other players even get their first shots! Here are the basics of how to lag*:

1 Use chalk or a stick to draw two parallel lines, a lag line and a pitch line, with about 10 feet of space between them.

*Some games may have their own special way, which we have included in the instructions for the game.

**2** Each player stands behind the pitch line and throws or shoots a marble towards the lag line, depending on what method is allowed for that game.

**3** The player whose marble is closest to the lag line, on either side of it, goes first.

In this book, the rules and scoring for each game are included in the instructions for that game. If you and your fellow players wish to change a rule to suit your abilities or playing conditions, these changes must be agreed to by everyone before the game begins.

## Are You Playing for Keeps?

Some players have favorite marbles—a lucky marble or perhaps an especially pretty one, or one that shoots well. If you know you are playing for keeps, only play with marbles you don't mind losing. Make sure you know whether you are playing for keeps (keepsies) or for fair (fairsies). If you are unsure, ask at the beginning of each game: Do I get my marbles back at the end of this game or could I lose them? If you know you are playing for keeps, only play with marbles you don't mind losing.

# Tournaments

Some people take their marbles seriously. If you are interested in playing marbles competitively, there are a number of ways to do this. You can organize a tournament in your area. Here's how to do it.

## Large Tournaments

1 Ask a local community center, parks board, or even a business if it would like to sponsor an event.

2 Advertise the event in your local newspaper, radio station, or television station. Local media may wish to create a special event around the marble tournament. Ask if any celebrities from the media want to participate in the event.

3 See if there is a marbles organization in your area that can give you more information.

## Small Tournaments

1 Ask your principal if you and your friends can have a tournament at your school.

2 You will need a printed set of rules for the tournament and instructions on how to play the game for the tournament.

## National Marbles Tournament

In the U.S., a National Marbles Tournament is held each year in Wildwood, New Jersey. Since 1922, children up to the age of 14 have entered this competition. Not everyone can play. In order to qualify for this competition, you have to have won a local tournament in your city, district, or state.

There are other tournaments you can enter. Check the Internet under Marble games for competitions in your area.

$3$ You will need a referee and scorer, whose job it is to interpret the rules and keep track of all the scores.

## Officials

When there's money and a trophy at stake, there's got to be an independent person or persons who can judge. The official can rule on such things as:

- size of marbles
- slips—when a player accidentally lets go of a marble and calls "Slips!" just as the marble leaves the player's hand
- what happens if a player moves before the marble enters the ring
- lifting a hand while shooting (histing) in a knuckles-down game, or other illegal shots
- correctness of the ring setup
- whether a shooter marble is in or out of the ring.

 When a shooter breaks, the official can approve another marble in its place. When the wind has moved a marble, the official returns it to its original position. The official also is the scorekeeper for the game.

## Penalties

The following penalties apply to Ringer tournaments:

- In a tournament, if a player lifts a hand when shooting, rearranges things, or touches the ground or moves forward while shooting, any marbles that previously had been knocked out by the player must be replaced and the player loses a turn.
- If a player changes shooters during a game, that player is disqualified.
- If a player talks to a coach during the game, or the coach signals the player during the game, the marbles the player has knocked out are put back on the center cross and the player must leave the area.
- There are no practice shots and no picking up marbles while they are moving.

# Supplies and Equipment

To play marbles, the basics are marbles, a surface to play on, and a marking tool, such as chalk or a stick. There are other things that are helpful to have, such as a marble bag and a marble mat, which you'll learn how to make in this book. So get the following together. You probably can find most of the supplies around the house:

- Marbles of different sizes. The ones that are $5/8$ inch (1.6 cm) in diameter are usually used for target marbles. Shooters are usually $1/2$ to $6/8$ inch (1.2 to 1.9 cm) in diameter. Steelies (ball bearings) or other metal marbles are allowed in most games except tournament Ringer.
- bag for carrying the marbles (see instructions for making a bag on page 34 for supplies needed for bag)
- piece of string about 6 feet (1.8 m) long to measure distances
- tape measure or yardstick
- piece of chalk or a stick to mark lines on the sidewalk or mark the ground
- piece of felt or other material about $2 \times 2$ inches ($5 \times 5$ cm) to rest your knuckles on when shooting
- paper or Styrofoam cups to make holes for Golf and gates for Croquet
- scissors
- felt pens
- cardboard box for games like Bridges
- shoe or sneaker for games like Puggy
- 10 x 10 foot (3 x 3 meter) piece of fabric, plastic or some old sheets, for making a marble mat (optional; see page 36)
- pencils
- masking tape to stick things together

## Collecting Marbles

If you were lucky enough to have a bag of marbles handed down to you by an older relative, you may have some valuable marbles in your collection. Old handmade marbles can be worth thousands of dollars, as collecting marbles has become a popular hobby. There are collectors all around the world who trade, buy, and sell these beautiful orbs. Some marbles are very valuable. Check with a local marble club or visit a marble collectors' show to learn more. Look in the library for books showing the many different kinds of marbles and their prices.

## Surfaces You Can Play On

Each game in this book lists some surfaces you can play on, for example:

- flat, smooth surface—sidewalk, asphalt, or other; flat floor of wood or linoleum; clay
- grass
- ground
- flat rugs or carpets
- marble mat

Serious marble players usually prefer concrete or other manmade surfaces as they are more reliable than grass or ground.

If you are playing outdoors on concrete or ground, your knees and knuckles can really get sore and scraped. You can use a piece of felt or another material such as cardboard on which you can rest your hand and knees. Your hand can't rest on thick material when you play, but your knees can rest on a scrap piece of rug.

*Note:* If you are playing on carpet, you can use your finger to trace a playing circle. You won't harm the carpet, and the line will disappear after it is vacuumed.

# Make a Marble Bag

So you don't lose your marbles, you can keep them in a marble bag. Here's an easy way to make a bag. You won't even need a sewing machine or any thread.

## You Will Need

- piece of strong fabric 10 x 10 inches (25 x 25 cm)
- round plate, slightly smaller than the fabric, such as a large salad plate or soup bowl, or a drawing compass
- scissors
- pencil or marker
- shoelace or colored cord
- hole punch

## What to Do

1 Place the fabric on a flat surface.

2 Put the plate on the center of the fabric and use a pencil to trace around the plate. This will give you a round circle, slightly smaller than the edge of the fabric.

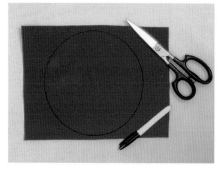

3 Cut out the circle.

4 Using a hole punch or scissors, poke holes ½ inch (1 cm) from the outer edge, spacing them about an inch apart. Get an adult to help you if you need help.

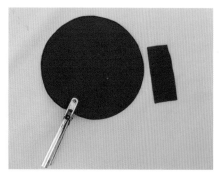

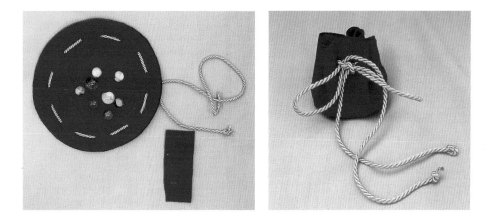

**5** Thread the shoelace through the holes, so it goes completely around the circle.

**6** Knot the ends of the shoelace together and pull on the lace to draw the material into a bag shape.

**7** Drop your marbles in and pull the cord closed. If you want a bigger marble bag, simply use a larger piece of material and make a bigger circle.

## Marble Webs

For the latest in marble games, prices, and trading information, check out the Internet. (Be sure you have permission to do this.) Using any search tools, type in MARBLES or HOBBIES. These words will lead you to any one of a growing number of Web sites. You'd be surprised to find out how many people share your interest in marbles. Discover the latest in games, all from the comfort of your own computer.

## Clubs

If you are interested in marbles, then how about joining a marble club or even starting your own club? Check the Internet or contact a marble trading group. These groups meet through the year. Some groups who trade in marbles do it "virtually" on the net.

## Make a Marble Mat

A marble mat is a special mat on which you can play marbles. It saves you time marking things as the distances are already marked. If you are playing on concrete, it can provide a smooth surface for your marbles to roll on.

### You Will Need

- large piece of thin fabric size 10 ft x 10 ft (3 x 3 m); two old bedsheets can be used, or even a large sheet of heavy plastic, such as a tarpaulin. It's best if it's not too slippery
- felt marker pens
- tape measure or yardstick
- 2 pencils
- 6-foot (180 cm) long piece of string
- helper

*Note:* you can sew two sheets together to create a piece of material large enough for the mat. Or poke around secondhand stores or garage sales and see if you can find an old round tablecloth. This would be perfect for a mat.

### What to Do

1 Place the sheet on a flat surface, like a wood floor or concrete pavement. Find the center of the piece of material by folding it in half both ways and creasing it at the center. Then unfold.

**2** Place the pointed end of one of the pencils at the center. If you are indoors, make sure you put a piece of cardboard, or even a flat plate, under the lead of the pencil so that it doesn't mark the floor.

**3** Tie one end of the long piece of string around the pencil and have a helper hold the pencil upright in the center of the material. Make sure the helper doesn't move the pencil. It stays in the same place while you draw all the circles. Measure the string from the pencil, so that it is slightly longer than 5 feet (1.5 m). Mark the 5-foot distance on the string and add 3 or 4 inches (7 to 10 cm); then cut off any excess string.

**4** Tie the loose end of the 5-foot string to the other pencil, so that you have a piece of string between the pencils that is exactly 5 feet long when it is stretched out straight.

**5** While your helper holds the pencil in the center of the material, pull your string taut and swing an arc so your pencil draws a circle on the material, the same way you would if you were using a compass. The 5-foot string will give you a circle with a 10-foot (305 cm) diameter. (The string is the radius of the circle; the diameter is always twice as big as the radius.)

**6** Shorten the string so that it is 4 feet (120 cm) long from pencil to pencil. Draw a circle of diameter 8 feet (240 cm) in the same way you drew the larger circle.

**7** Shorten the string to 3 feet (90 cm) and draw a circle of diameter 6 feet (180 cm).

**8** Shorten the string to 2 feet (60 cm) and draw a circle of diameter 4 feet (120 cm).

**9** Shorten the string to 18 inches (45 cm) and draw a circle of diameter 3 feet (90 cm).

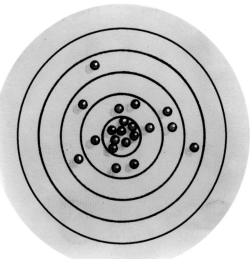

Drawing the 1-foot circle.                    The finished mat.

**10** Shorten the string to 1 foot (30 cm) and draw a circle of diameter 2 feet (60 cm).

**11** For the last circle, shorten the string to 6 inches (15 cm) and draw the circle of diameter 1 foot, the innermost circle on the mat.

**12** Trace along the lines of the circles using different-colored felt markers that can be seen clearly on your fabric. You may wish to label each circle with its size in feet.

**13** Draw a cross in the center of the circles using the foldlines as a guide and a ruler. The cross lines should reach the 2-foot circle.

**14** Take the marble mat with you when you are playing marbles. You will not need to measure anything, and you will have a smooth playing surface.

# GAMES

# Ringer

*This is, according to purists, the only game of marbles. Ringer is the official game played at marble tournaments and championships. For a competition, only two players can play at one time. In a regular game, from 2 to 6 can play. In a tournament game, all play is for fair. Marbles are returned to their owners at the end of the game.*

**THE OFFICIAL RULES:** tournament
**PLAYING SURFACE:** smooth, level
ground or hard clay; flat marble mat
**TECHNIQUE:** knuckles down

## Setup

1 The ring (playing circle) must be exactly 10 feet (305 cm) in diameter.

2 Draw a cross that intersects in the middle of the ring. Place 7 marbles down the cross, each marble 3 inches (7.5 cm) away from the next one, with the center marble on the center of the cross. Place 6 marbles across, 3 on each side of the center marble; each marble is 3 inches (7.5 cm) away from the nearest marble on the cross.

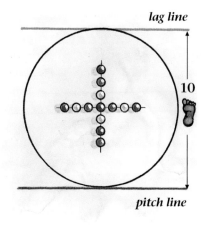

3 Create a lag line by drawing a line so that it just touches the edge of the ring.

**4** Directly opposite from the lag line, draw a pitch line, parallel to the lag line, so that it just touches the opposite edge of the ring.

**5** Target marbles must be made of glass and measure $5/8$ inch in diameter. Shooters may be of any material except metal and may not be smaller than $1/2$ inch or bigger than $6/8$ inch in diameter.

## How to play

**1** Each player stands toeing the pitch line or knuckling down on it, and shoots or tosses a marble towards the lag line. The player whose marble comes closest to the lag line, on either side of it, goes first. The others follow in the order that their shooters were nearest the lag line.

**2** The marble that you use to lag is the marble you must use to shoot with in the game.

**3** All shots must be taken with knuckles down, so that at least one knuckle is in contact with the ground, and the player must hold this position until the shooter has left the player's hand.

**4** At the start of the game, each player in turn knuckles down at any point he or she chooses outside the ring line and shoots his or her marble into the ring. The object of the game is to knock a target marble or opponent's shooter from the ring, or hit them, while leaving the player's own shooter inside the ring.

**5** If a player knocks a marble or marbles out of the ring, or hits his opponent's shooter, or knocks his opponent's shooter out of the ring, he can keep shooting, as long as his own shooter stays in the ring. After his first miss, he stops shooting and adds up his score. Then it's the next player's turn.

**6** If a player's shooter is in the ring after he misses, it stays there, and his opponents can shoot at it.

**7** If a shooter rolls out of the ring, the player picks it up and on his next shot may shoot from any point on the ring line.

**8** The game ends when the last marble is shot out.

### SCORING

**1** Each marble knocked out of the ring is worth a point. The first player to get 7 points wins.

**2** Each time a player hits an opponent's shooter and doesn't knock it out of the ring, the player gets a point.

**3** Each time a player knocks an opponent's shooter out of the ring, the player is credited with all the marbles scored up to then by the opponent.

**4** An opponent whose shooter is knocked out of the ring is out of the game ("killed").

# Bombers

*No one has to run for cover in this friendly game of Bombers. For 2 players.*

**PLAYING SURFACE:** grass, ground, rug, or marble mat

**TECHNIQUE:** bowling, tossing

## Setup

Draw a pitch line.

## How to play

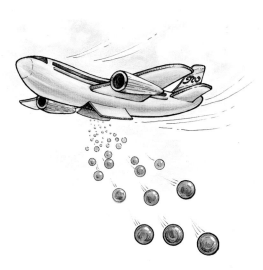

1 Player 1 pitches or tosses a marble any distance. This is the target marble.

2 Player 2 tries to hit the target marble by bowling a marble towards it.

3 If Player 2's thrown marble is within a handspan of or hits the target marble, the target marble belongs to Player 2.

4 Player 1 then tosses down another marble on the ground as in Step 1, and Player 2 holds a marble at eye level and tries to drop or bomb the marble on top of Player 1's marble ("bombing"). If Player 2's marble bomb misses, Player 1 keeps the target marble.

5 If in Step 3, Player 2's marble is not within a handspan of the target, both players get their marbles back and start again.

6 After Player 2 has had a turn being the bomber, the players trade places and start again.

### PENALTY

If player bends or stoops during bombing, the player has to take the shot again, this time dropping the marble from eye level.

# Bounce Eye

*This is a simple game, perfect
for a younger player, who is
also closer to the ground.
For 2 or more players.*

**PLAYING SURFACE:** ground, grass, rug,
 or marble mat
**TECHNIQUE:** dropping, bombsies

## Setup

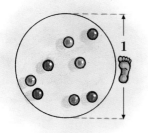

1 Draw a circle 1 foot (30 cm) across,
or use a shoestring as the radius of your
circle.

2 Each player scatters an equal number of marbles inside the circle.

## How to play

1 Players take turns trying to hit a marble
by dropping a shooter (taw) onto it, while
standing outside the circle.

2 Each shot must be dropped from eye
level—no bending or stooping.

3 If a player fails to knock out a marble,
the player's taw is added to the marbles in
the circle. Then it is the next player's turn.

4 The game is over when there are no
marbles left in the circle.

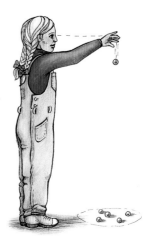

### SCORING
Any marble knocked out on a shot belongs to the player who knocked
it out. The person with the most marbles at the end of the game wins.

# Bull's-Eye

*This game is like playing darts with marbles.
A game for 2 to 4 players.*

**PLAYING SURFACE:** ground or smooth,
flat surface; marble mat
**TECHNIQUE:** knuckles down

## Setup

**1** Draw 4 circles, one inside the other. Make
the smallest circle of 1 foot (30 cm) diameter,
the others of diameter 2, 3, and 4 feet (60,
90, and 120 cm).

**2** In each circle, mark the number of points
you will earn if your marble lands in that circle. (See boxes in setup diagram.)

**3** Draw a shooting line 6 feet (180 cm) away
from the outer edge of the largest circle.

## How to play

**1** Start with no marbles in the circles.

**2** Each player takes a turn shooting 3 marbles at the bull's-eye from
the shooting line. The player gains the point value of the area of the
circle that the marble lands in for that shot.

**3** The other players tally the shooting player's score for the three shots.

**4** If a player knocks a marble out of the circle, that marble's score
does not count.

**5** At the end of the turn, the player removes all 3 marbles and the
next player goes.

**6** Determine how many turns are to be taken to finish a game.

**SCORING**
The player with the highest score at the end of the game wins.

# Castles
## or Pyramid

*There's an old saying that your home is your castle. That saying also applies to marbles. A game for 2 or more players.*

**PLAYING SURFACE:** ground or smooth, flat surface; marble mat
**TECHNIQUE:** any method

## GAME 1

### Setup

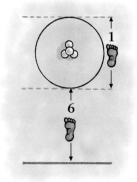

1 Each player takes a turn building a castle or pyramid by placing three marbles as a base and one on top. The builder is the keeper of the castle. If you are playing for higher stakes, build a larger castle by increasing the number of marbles on the base and top.

2 Draw a 1-foot (30 cm) circle or use the center circle of the marble mat.

3 Draw a line 6 feet (180 cm) away from the circle. This is the shooting line.

## How to play

1 The players, except for the keeper, take turns shooting a marble at the castle.

2 Any marbles knocked out of the circle belong to the player who knocked them out.

3 The keeper rebuilds the castle each time it is knocked down, replacing any marbles knocked out of the circle with his or her own marbles.

4 Any player's marbles left in the circle after every opponent has had a turn belong to the keeper.

5 After each player has had a turn shooting at the castle, trade places. A new keeper now makes the castle and each of the other players takes a turn.

### SCORING

After each player has built a castle and all players have shot, the player who has gained the most marbles wins.

## GAME 2

### Setup

1 Players build their four-marbled castles an agreed-upon distance away from each other.

### How to play

1 Each player takes a turn shooting marbles at the opponents' castles. Players decide how many turns each will have.

2 If a player knocks down a castle, all the castle marbles belong to the player, including the marble that was the shooter.

3 The keeper keeps any marbles that miss his castle or fail to knock it down.

### SCORING

The player with the most marbles at the end of the turns wins.

### Just for fun

If you are at home and have no one to play marbles with, try this: Create your own marble castle or pyramid. Like building a house of cards, this will require a steady hand and a stable building surface—a thick rug works very well.

# Chasies
## or Lawn Bowling

*No marble-shooting skill needed, just a good eye and a steady arm.*
*Small children can also play, but only if they are old enough not to*
*put marbles in their mouths. For 2 or more players.*

**PLAYING SURFACE:** grass or ground
**TECHNIQUE:** tossing, bowling

## How to play

1 Place a large marble on
the playing area.

2 Players take 10 running steps
away in any direction from this marble.

3 Each player tosses or bowls a marble towards the target marble in
turn. Any player who hits the target marble wins automatically.

4 After each person has thrown a marble, see where each person's
marble has landed. The person whose marble is within a handspan of
the target marble wins the target marble. The next person puts down a
new marble to be the target marble.

5 If no one is within a handspan, each player whose marble is within
3 feet (about 1 meter) of the target gets another turn by standing over
the target marble and trying to hit it by dropping or bombing his or
her marble on top of it. All drops must be from waist height.

6 If the target marble is hit, the next player puts down a new target
marble and the game starts all over again. If no one hits the target
marble, then the marbles stays in the field for the next game of
Chasies.

**SCORING**
Whoever gets the most marbles wins.

# Die Shot

*Dice are usually used in gambling games or games of chance. Here's a way to shoot dice that requires skill instead of luck.*

**PLAYING SURFACE:** ground, or smooth, flat surface
**TECHNIQUE:** any method

## Setup

### GAME 1

1 Push a marble just slightly into the ground or playing surface to keep it from rolling.

2 Balance a die on the marble.

## How to play

1 Each player takes a turn being the keeper.

2 A player pays the keeper one marble for the right to shoot at the die marble from a distance agreed upon by all players.

3 If the player knocks the die from the marble, the keeper pays that player the same number of marbles as there are dots on the top of the die.

4 If the player misses the die marble, the keeper owns the shot marble.

## GAME 2

Instead of using one marble to balance
the die on, place three marbles down and
balance the die on top of the three marbles. Play the game the same as before.

## OPTION

Try playing the game backwards. Roll the die.
Place the marble on the die and take turns
shooting at the die. If the marble is knocked
off the die, the player who shot receives payment equal to the number showing on the
top of the die.

# Dobblers

*This is an easy game to set up and play.
For 2 to 4 players.*

**PLAYING SURFACE:** ground; smooth,
flat surface; marble mat
**TECHNIQUE:** knuckles down

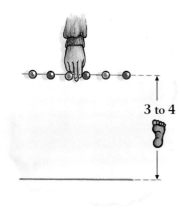

3 to 4

## Setup

1 Each player puts an agreed-upon number of marbles into the pot to serve as target marbles.

2 Draw a line and place the target marbles along the line, leaving two finger spaces between marbles.

3 Draw a shooting line about 3 or 4 feet (a meter or 120 cm) away from and parallel to the marble line.

## How to play

1 Each player takes a turn shooting at the target marbles from behind the shooting line.

2 If you miss a shot, your shooter stays where it is. Take your next shot from where your shooter lies.

3 If another player hits your shooter, you must add another marble to the target marbles on the line.

4 If you hit a target marble, it belongs to you.

### SCORING
The player with the most marbles at the end wins.

# Double Ring Taw

## or Increase Pound

*Double Ring Taw is one of the oldest marble games.*
*For 2 or more players.*

**PLAYING SURFACE:** ground, smooth surface, or marble mat
**TECHNIQUE:** knuckles down

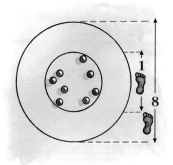

### Setup

1 Draw a circle about 1 foot in diameter (30 cm) or use the smallest circle on the marble mat. This circle is the "pound."

2 Draw another circle around the first one, about 8 feet (240 cm) in diameter, or use the 8-foot circle on the marble mat. The large circle is the shooting line.

## How to play

1 Each player puts in 4 or 5 marbles, which are scattered in the pound.

2 Each player takes a turn shooting a marble at the target marbles from the edge of the 8-foot circle. If a player knocks a marble out of the pound and his shooter leaves the pound, the marble is his, and his turn ends.

**3** If your shooter ends up in the pound, you must add one marble to the pound before removing your shooter.

**4** If your shooter ends up inside the 8-foot circle but outside the pound, you must leave it there; it becomes a target marble too.

**5** If your shooter ends up outside both circles, you can shoot from anywhere outside the 8-foot circle on your next turn.

**6** If another player successfully hits your shooter, you have to give that player one marble.

### SCORING

When all the target marbles have been knocked from the pound, the person with the most marbles wins.

# Dropsies

*A game for 2 to 4 players. Instead of a circle, this time you get to use a square.*

**PLAYING SURFACE:** any surface outdoors, or rug or marble mat
**TECHNIQUE:** dropping

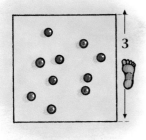

## Setup

1 Draw a 3-foot (90 cm) square.

2 Each player puts 4 or 5 marbles inside the square.

## How to play

1 Stand with feet outside of the edge of the square. Players take turns dropping a marble from waist height onto the marbles inside the square.

2 Keep any marble you knock out of the square. As long as your shooter stays in the square when you hit another marble, it is your turn.

3 It is your opponent's turn when you don't hit anything or your shooter rolls outside the square.

**SCORING**
The first player to hit 5 marbles out wins.

# Eggs in the Bush

*This is a game of marbles that anyone can play.*
*For 2 or more players.*

**PLAYING SURFACE:** your hand
**TECHNIQUE:** none

## How to play

1 Place any number of marbles, from 1 to 5, in your hand.

2 Your opponent guesses how many marbles you are holding. If you have tiny hands you may wish to keep your hands behind your back while the other players are guessing.

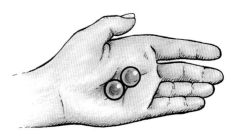

### SCORING

1 If your opponent guesses correctly, pay her the number of marbles in your hand. If your opponent guesses the wrong number, she gives you the difference between the number in your hand and the number she guessed.

## EXAMPLES

1 You have 3 marbles in your hand. Your opponent guesses "3." You give her 3 marbles.

**2** You have 3 marbles in your hand. Your opponent guesses "1." Your opponent gives you 2 marbles.

**3** You have 3 marbles in your hand. Your opponent guesses "5." Your opponent gives you 2 marbles.

## Only for the daring: Double or nothing

Let's say your opponent guessed correctly. Hold your hands straight out and ask which hand the marbles are in. If the opponent correctly guesses which hand, you give her twice the number of marbles in your hand. If your opponent guesses incorrectly, she gets nothing.

## Game hints

- Do not clench or squeeze the fist holding the marbles, as it is easier for someone to guess how many marbles you are holding if you do.
- The smaller the fist, the fewer marbles a player's hand is holding.
- In the double or nothing game, hold both your fists as loosely as possible.
- When guessing which hand your opponent is holding the marbles in, always choose the hand that is more tightly closed.

# Football

*How about a game of football played in your own backyard? No, you don't need a huge field, just your imagination and some marbles. For 1 to 5 players.*

**PLAYING SURFACE:** smooth, flat surface or marble mat
**TECHNIQUE:** any method

## Setup

1 Draw a line 3 to 4 feet (1 meter to 120 cm) long.

2 Use chalk to make two curves around the center line so that the area is a football shape.

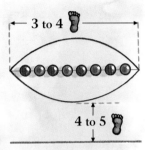

3 Draw a taw line (shooting line) 4 or 5 feet (120 to 150 cm) away from the curve.

## How to play

1 Have each player contribute an equal number of marbles and place them along the center line.

2 Players stand behind the taw line and take turns trying to shoot a target marble off the center line and out of the football. Each player gets one shot per turn.

3 Marbles that are hit but don't move out of the football are "dead" or out of play, and go back to their owners at the end of the game.

4 The game continues until all the marbles are out of the football.

### SCORING

1 Marbles hit out of the football go to the player that hit them out.

2 The person who has the most marbles at the end of the game wins.

# Forts

## or Fortress

*The setup for this game also can be used for Bull's-Eye. For 2 or more players.*

**PLAYING SURFACE:** ground; smooth, flat surface; marble mat
**TECHNIQUE:** knuckles down

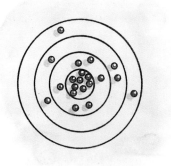

## Setup

1 Draw 4 circles, one inside the other. Make the smallest one 2 feet (60 cm) in diameter, and the next ones 4, 6, and 8 feet (120, 180, and 240 cm) in diameter (see diagram). The center circle is called the fort.

2 Each player puts 1 marble in the outer circle, 2 in the next circle, 3 in the third, and 4 in the center circle. These marbles should be randomly spaced around the circles.

## How to play

Players must shoot at the target marbles in order: the marbles in the outer circle are the first target marbles, followed by the marbles in the 6-foot circle, the 4-foot circle, and finally in the innermost circle. Players work to clear each circle before going on to the next one.

1 Each player starts shooting at a target marble in the outermost circle from a distance of at least 2 feet (60 cm) away, anywhere around the circle.

**2** When you hit a target marble in the correct circle, it is yours, and your turn is over. You do not have to knock it out of the circle to claim the marble.

**3** If you miss a marble or hit a marble in the wrong circle, you must pay one shooter into the fort and your turn is over.

**4** You must leave your shooter where it lands and take your next shot from there if it is in a circle.

**5** Players may shoot at other players' shooters, but don't keep them if they hit them.

**6** If a player hits a target marble in the 4-foot ring, she gets a second shot.

**7** If a player hits a marble in the fort, she can get an extra turn, and a second extra turn if she hits another marble out of the fort.

**8** The game is over when the fort is empty.


### SCORING
When the fort is empty, each player sees how many marbles she has gained. The player who has gained the most wins.

# Golf

*You won't need a set of clubs or membership at a golf course to play this game.*
*For 2 or more players.*

**PLAYING SURFACE:** ground
**TECHNIQUE:** rolling, tossing, bowling

## Setup

## GAME 1

**1** Dig a row of up to 18 shallow holes in the ground. The holes can be of different widths.

**2** Number the holes 1 through 18.

**3** Draw a shooting line a few feet away.

**4** Each player puts an equal number of marbles into the pot.

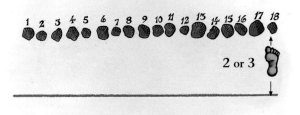

Game 1

## How to play

**1** Each player takes a turn trying to shoot a marble into the first hole.

**2** If you miss a hole, your shooter stays where it is, and you shoot from this place on your next turn.

**3** Write down the number of shots it takes to get your marble in the hole. Keep score for each hole.

**4** Once you get into the first hole, go on to the next one. Just like a real game of golf, at the end of the game, the person with the lowest score wins all the marbles in the pot.

## GAME 2

**1** Instead of digging the holes in a straight line, space them out around the area and create mounds, water traps, and sand traps in front of each hole.

**2** Give each hole a number on a small piece of paper stuck near it. Give each its own shooting line. Vary the distances between the shooting lines and holes so the line is between 10 and 20 feet (3 and 6 m) from the hole.

**3** Play the game as described above for Game 1.

Game 2

# Hundreds

*This is a game for 2 players. You play until*
*one person gets 100 points.*

**PLAYING SURFACE:** ground or flat, smooth surface, or marble mat
**TECHNIQUE:** knuckles down

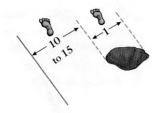

## Setup

1 Make a shallow hole in the ground, about a foot (30 cm) across, or draw a circle that size on the playing surface. (On the marble mat, use the 1-foot circle.)

2 Draw a shooting line 10 to 15 feet (3 to 4.5 m) away.

## How to play

1 Players take turns standing behind the line and trying to get a marble into the circle (or hole).

2 Each time you get your marble in the circle (or hole), you get 10 points and shoot again.

3 Keep shooting until you miss; then it is the other player's turn. Take your shooter back.

### SCORING
The first player to get 10 shots in the hole (100 points) is the winner.

# Knuckle Box

*This is a game similar to Dropsies, except you shoot marbles instead of dropping them. For 2 or more players.*

**PLAYING SURFACE:** ground or grass; smooth surface or marble mat
**TECHNIQUE:** knuckles down

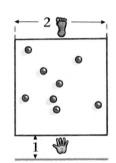

## Setup

1 Draw a 2-foot (60 x 60 cm) square (the box).

2 Each player scatters 4 or more marbles into the square.

3 Measure one handspan away from the square and draw a line as a shooting line. (You can make your line on any side of the square you want, or move around.)

## How to play

1 Each player takes a turn shooting a marble from the shooting line, trying to hit a marble out while having the shooter remain in the box.

2 If your marble knocks out a target marble from the square, and your shooter also rolls out, keep the target marble, but your turn is over.

3 If your marble knocks out a target marble, but stays in the square, keep the target marble and shoot again from one handspan outside the box. If you miss, take your shooter and your turn ends.

4 If your shooter rolls into the box and hits nothing, it remains there.

### SCORING
When the square is empty, the player who gained the most marbles wins.

# Lagout

## or Rebound

*This is a game you can play by yourself when no one is around, or you can gather a group to compete. This is a great game for younger players as it requires little skill.*

**PLAYING SURFACE**: ground, grass, or flat surface near wall

**TECHNIQUE**: tossing

## Setup

1 Find a smooth wall. Brick or other really rough surfaces aren't recommended as the texture affects the marble's bounce.

Game 1

## How to play

### GAME 1

1 Each player throws one marble at the wall, so that it bounces off and lands anywhere in the playing area. Marbles are left where they fall.

2 Players then take turns throwing a marble so that it hits the wall and bounces to land on a previously thrown marble.

3 The first player to hit another marble collects all the other marbles on the playing area and the game starts again.

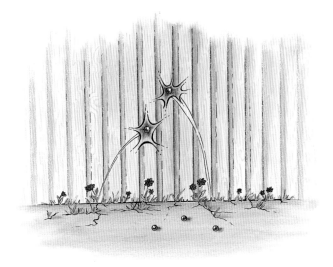

# GAME 2

1 Each player places a marble on a line drawn 2 feet (60 cm) away from the wall.

2 Draw another line 3 feet (90 cm) away from the first line.

3 Players take turns shooting a marble, knuckles down, from the 3-foot line, so that the marble first hits the wall and then rebounds into a marble on the 2-foot line.

4 The first player to hit a marble on the line wins all the marbles on the line.

5 If a player misses a marble, he takes the next shot from wherever the shooter landed on the previous shot.

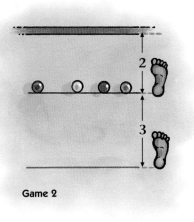

Game 2

# Long Taw

*What is a taw and why is it long?*
*A taw is a shooter.*
*In this case it's long because you're far away*
*from the target marble.*
*For 2 players.*

**PLAYING SURFACE:** ground or smooth, flat surface; tile
**TECHNIQUE:** knuckles down

## Setup

1 Draw a line 12 feet (360 cm) long. Mark off the 6-foot (180 cm) spot on the line. Place a marble at the 6-foot spot while your opponent places a marble at the 12-foot spot.

2 Draw a taw line (shooting line) perpendicular to the start of your 12-foot line, at the end with no marble.

## How to play

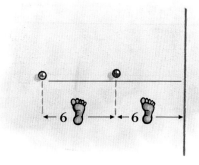

1 Players take turns being the first player in a round. All shooting is from behind the taw line.

2 Player 1 shoots at the nearest marble. If she hits it, she keeps it and shoots at the furthest marble. If she hits it, she keeps it and that round ends.

**3** If Player 1 misses on either try, she leaves her shooter where it lands, and Player 2 can shoot at her shooter or at any of the other marbles. If Player 1's shooter is hit, Player 2 wins all the marbles.

**4** If Player 2 misses any marbles, her shooter stays where it landed and Player 1 gets a chance at hitting it.

**5** The round is over when no marbles are left on the ground.

**6** The next round begins; this time Player 2 goes first.

**SCORING**

Whoever wins the most rounds wins the game.

# Losing Your Marbles

*A tossing game for 2 or more players. You may think the title of this game really sums up what playing marbles is all*

**PLAYING SURFACE:** ground
**TECHNIQUE:** tossing

## Setup

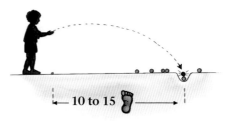

1 Dig a hole about 6 inches (15 cm) wide and 2 inches deep (5 cm) in the ground.

← 10 to 15 →

2 Draw a shooting line, or in this case a tossing line, 10 to 15 feet (3 to 4.5 m) away from the hole.

3 One player puts a target marble in the hole.

## How to play

1 Players take turns trying to toss a marble into the hole to hit a target marble inside.

2 If a player misses the hole, the marble stays where it lands.

3 The first player to hit a marble in the hole 3 times wins all the marbles on the ground that missed the hole.

4 The next player puts a target marble in the hole and the players repeat steps 1 to 3.

### SCORING
The player who has won the most marbles wins the game.

# Milkie

## or Old Bowler

*Folklore says that Abraham Lincoln was an excellent marble player and this was his favorite game. It's called Milkie because of the white marble. A game for 4 players.*

**PLAYING SURFACE:** ground
**TECHNIQUE:** knuckles down

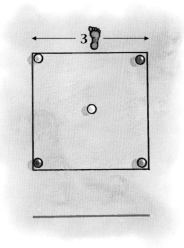

## Setup

**1** Draw a 3-foot (90 x 90 cm) square or whatever size you like. Place a clear or white marble in the center of the square. This marble is called the old bowler.

**2** Draw a taw line (shooting line) outside the square, as far away as all players agree on.

**3** Each player places one marble in a corner of the square.

## How to play

**1** Players take turns shooting at the corner marbles from behind the taw line.

**2** The player who is shooting chooses another player's marble as the target and tells the other 3 players which marble is to be hit.

**3** The shooting player (Player A) must hit the center marble in such a way that the center marble then hits the named corner marble out of the square.

**4** When the center marble hits the target marble out, the center marble itself must stay in the square.

**5** If Player A succeeds in Step 3, she can continue shooting at the corner marbles until she misses.

**6** If Player A misses the marble in the center, or if the marble in the center misses the named corner marble, one of two things can happen:

● The owner of the corner marble (Player B) can try to get back at Player A by shooting Player A's marble far out of the playing area. Player B then moves her own marble back to her corner. Player A, whose marble has just been shot out of the square, must now shoot the displaced marble back to its original corner position.

● Player B can choose not to shoot at Player A's marble. Then Player A puts her marble back in its original corner, and the next player shoots.

### SCORING

When the center marble hits a player's marble out of the square, the player loses that marble. The winner is the player whose marble is left at the end of the game.

# Newark Killer

*This game was invented years ago in Newark, New Jersey.
For 2 or more players.*

**PLAYING SURFACE:** smooth, flat surface or marble mat
**TECHNIQUE:** any method

## Setup

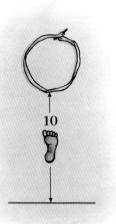

1 Use a shoelace to make a small circle, or use the smallest circle on the marble mat.

2 Draw a shooting line 10 feet (3 m) away, or make a line touching the outermost ring on the marble mat.

3 Each player sets aside 10 marbles. It's a good idea to choose marbles you don't mind losing.

## How to play

1 Each player takes turns trying to shoot or roll a marble into the shoelace circle or small circle from behind the shooting line.

2 After all the players have shot all 10 marbles, the player with the most marbles in the circle becomes the "killer."

3 The killer shoots at any opponent's marble outside of the circle. If he hits it, he keeps it and continues shooting from the place his shooter ended up on the previous shot. When the killer misses, the game ends.

**SCORING**

Each marble a player shoots into the small circle counts as a point. If your marble gets knocked out of the circle by another player, you lose a point. If it gets knocked in, you get a point. The killer automatically wins the game.

# Odds or Evens

*Like Eggs in the Bush, a guessing game that anyone can play.*
*For 2 or more players.*

**PLAYING SURFACE:** your hand
**TECHNIQUE:** none

## Setup

1 One person, the questioner, places any number of marbles from 1 to 5 in her hand.

2 The questioner asks each player in turn whether she is holding an even or odd number of marbles. (If the questioner has tiny hands, she may wish to keep her hands behind her back while the other players are guessing.)

3 After each player guesses, the questioner shows the players how many marbles are in her hand. Players who guessed wrong give the questioner a marble. Players who guessed right get a marble from the questioner.

4 Each player takes a turn being questioner.

**SCORING**
Whoever gets the most marbles wins.

# Picking Plums

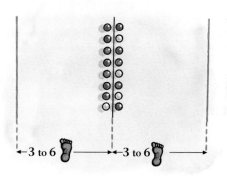

*These plums are fun to pick, so grab your shooter. A game for a small number of players, who play as teams.*

**PLAYING SURFACE:** smooth, flat surface or marble mat
**TECHNIQUE:** any method

## Setup

**1** Draw a plum line 3 to 4 feet (1 meter to 120 cm) long, or use the center line on the marble mat.

**2** Draw a taw (shooting) line on either side of the plum line, about 3 to 6 feet (90 to 180 cm) away from it.

**3** Each player puts in at least 4 marbles, depending on the number of players. You should have at least 16 marbles to begin the game.

**4** Divide into two teams. Each team will shoot from behind one taw line.

**5** Divide the marbles in half. Place your team's marbles along the side of the plum line that is farthest from you, with about 2 fingers' distance between each marble and the next one.

## How to play

1 Each team gets 3 shots per turn (1 player goes per turn) to try to hit the opposing team's marbles over the plum line.

2 A target marble knocked over the line belongs to the team that hit it.

3 After each shot, each player collects his shooter and any marbles hit.

**SCORING**
The first team to knock all the opposing team's plums over the line wins.

# Poison Ring

*There are several versions of this game.*
*For 2 or more players.*

**PLAYING SURFACE:** smooth ground or marble mat
**TECHNIQUE:** knuckles down

## Setup

**1** Dig a small hole in the ground or draw a circle about 8 inches to 1 foot (20 to 30 cm) in diameter. If you are using the marble mat, use the smallest circle. This is called the poison ring.

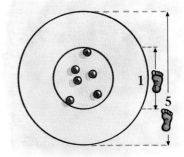

**2** Each player scatters 3 or 4 marbles in the poison ring.

**3** Draw another circle, about 5 feet (150 cm) in diameter, around the first circle.

**4** To decide who's first, each player takes a turn bowling a marble from 5 feet away from the outer ring. The player whose marble is closest to the poison ring's outer edge, but not actually inside in the ring, shoots first.

## How to play

**1** A player can shoot from anywhere along the outside of the ring. The object is to knock a marble from the poison ring and leave the shooter inside the large ring, but not in the poison ring.

**2** The player shooting claims any marble he knocks outside the poison ring.

**3** If the player shooting misses a target marble, or if the shooter stays inside the poison ring, the player puts back all the marbles he won so far in the game. If the player failed to win any marbles that round, the player pays the poison ring 2 marbles.

**4** If the player's marble lands inside the poison ring, it becomes part of the ring.

**5** If a player knocks his shooter and some marbles out of the poison ring, his shooter is "poisonous." When it's his next turn, he can shoot at other player's shooters, which are "poisoned" if he hits them.

**6** If a marble is hit by a "poisoned" shooter, the marble's owner has to leave the game with the marbles he has won so far.

**7** The "poisonous" player stays poisoned until he misses another player's shooter or has to pay marbles into the poison ring.

**8** The game ends when all the marbles are shot out of the poison ring, or when only one player is left. He wins all the remaining marbles in the poison ring.

### SCORING

The last player, or the one who has gotten the most marbles, wins.

# Potsies

*The winner gets to keep all the marbles. Only play this game if you are prepared for the consequences! For 2 or 3 players.*

**PLAYING SURFACE:** smooth, flat surface
**TECHNIQUE:** knuckles down

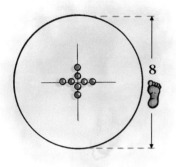

## Setup

**1** Draw a circle 8 feet (240 cm) in diameter or use the 8-foot circle on the marble mat.

**2** Each player contributes an equal number of marbles to the pot. Arrange them in the center of the circle in a cross.

## How to play

**1** Lag to see who goes first.

**2** Each player takes a turn shooting a marble from outside the ring. The object is to knock a marble from the cross out of the circle, leaving your shooter in the circle.

**3** If your shooter rolls out of the ring in addition to the target marble, you have to replace the target marble in the same position it was in before you hit it, and your turn is over.

**4** If you are successful in knocking out a target marble while keeping your shooter inside the ring, you may shoot again, from wherever your shooter ended up.

### SCORING

**1** Any marble shot out of the ring while your shooter stays in the ring goes into your pile.

**2** The first person to win more marbles than she originally gave in to the pot wins the whole pot.

# Potty

*This game requires a steady hand and a good eye.*
*For 2 or more players.*

**PLAYING SURFACE:** ground or marble mat
**TECHNIQUE:** any method

## Setup

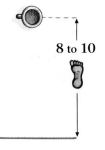

8 to 10

1 Dig a shallow hole, or use an object with a hole in it, such as a metal cup or a shoe, as the potty.

2 Draw a shooting line about 8 to 10 feet (2.5 to 3 m) away from the hole.

3 Lag to see who goes first by throwing marbles at the potty. Whoever gets closest without having his marble go in the potty is first.

## How to play

1 Players take turns tossing or shooting their marbles at the potty. The goal is to get your marble inside the potty, or as close as possible.

2 The first player getting a marble into the potty (we'll call him Player A) collects all the marbles that are within a handspan of the potty (but see #5 before collecting marbles).

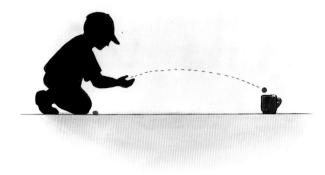

**3** All the marbles beyond a handspan of the potty are given back to the players who tossed them.

**4** If a player is skilled enough to get a marble in on the first toss, when there are no other marbles on the playing field, each opponent gives that player one marble as payment.

**5** Before Player A can collect all the marbles within a handspan of the potty, the next player to shoot (Player B) has 3 tries to hit Player A's marble by bombsies. Player B stands over Player A's marble and drops a marble. If Player B is successful, he gets all the marbles within a handspan of the potty, instead of Player A.

### SCORING

The winner is the player with the most marbles at the end of an agreed-to number of rounds.

# Puggy

*There are several versions of this game. Here are two.*
*Try them both and see which one you like better.*
*For 2 or more players.*

**PLAYING SURFACE:** ground or smooth surface or marble mat
**TECHNIQUE:** knuckles down

## GAME 1

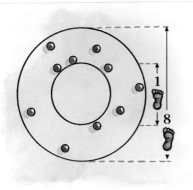

### Setup

1 Dig a hole 6 inches (15 cm) to a foot (30 cm) in diameter. This is the puggy. Or draw a circle on a flat surface as the puggy if you can't dig a hole.

2 Draw a large circle around the first one, about 8 feet (240 cm) in diameter.

## How to play

1 Each player contributes an equal number of marbles. Scatter the marbles in the area between the two circles. None should be in the inner circle.

2 Take turns shooting at the target marbles from the outside of the large circle. If you knock a target marble into the puggy, that marble is yours. Take your shooter and shoot again from outside the large ring.

3 If the player doesn't hit any marbles into the puggy, he takes his shooter and his turn is over.

4 If a player's shooter rolls into the puggy while knocking in a target marble, the target marble goes back in the circle and the player's turn ends.

**SCORING**

When all the target marbles have been knocked into the puggy, the person with the most marbles wins.

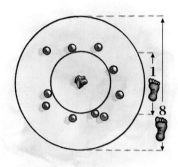

## GAME 2

### Setup

**1** Draw a circle 8 feet (240 cm) in diameter or use the 8-foot marker on the marble mat. This is your shooting line.

**2** Place an object like a shoe or a rock in the center of the large circle to be the puggy.

## How to play

**1** Each player contributes an equal number of marbles to the pot.

**2** Scatter the marbles about a foot (30 cm) from the puggy.

**3** Take turns shooting your marble at the target marbles from outside the large circle. If you knock a target marble into the puggy, that marble is yours. Take your shooter and shoot again from the outside ring's edge.

**SCORING**

When all the target marbles have been knocked into the puggy, the person with the most marbles wins.

# Rockies
## or Crackers

*This is a perfect game for a cracked sidewalk.*
*For 2 or more players.*

**PLAYING SURFACE:** sidewalk
**TECHNIQUE:** any method

## Setup

1 Choose a rough sidewalk area with cracks and bumps.

2 The player in charge of the marble places a marble somewhere on the sidewalk where it will be hard to hit and offers a large number of marbles as a prize for any player who can hit the target marble.

## How to play

Players take turns shooting from a line every one agrees on, about 10 feet (3 m) away from the target marble.

### SCORING

If the player misses, his shooter belongs to the player in charge. If the player hits the target marble, the player in charge must pay the prize to the player that hit the marble, and the game ends.

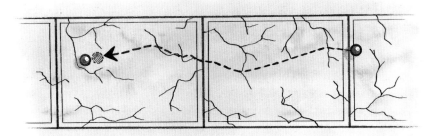

# Spangy

*This game must be played with 5 players. Different versions of this game have been played for the last 150 years.*

**PLAYING SURFACE:** ground or smooth surface
**TECHNIQUE:** any method

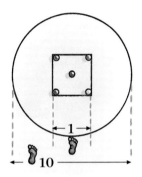

## Setup

**1** Draw a 1-foot (30 cm) square.

**2** Each player contributes a marble. Place a marble in each corner and one in the center of the square. These are the target marbles.

**3** Draw a circle of diameter 10 feet (3 m) around the square.

## How to play

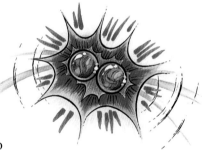

**1** Each player takes a turn trying to knock a target marble out of the square, shooting from outside the circle.

**2** If a player hits the marble from the square, the marble belongs to him and he continues shooting.

**3** If a player misses the marble, the shooter stays where it landed and becomes one of the target marbles.

**4** If your shooter lands within a handspan of any target marble, you may "span" the marbles. Open your hand wide. Place your thumb next to the shooter and your pinkie or another finger next to the target marble. With one motion, close your hand in such a manner that the marbles knock together. If you can do this, both marbles belong to you. If you miss, you lose your shooter.

### SCORING

When the square is cleared of all the target marbles, the player with the most marbles wins.

# Spanners

## or Handspan

*A handspan is the distance between the end of your thumb and the end of another finger, such as your pinkie, when you open your hand as wide as it can go. Kids who play piano can usually stretch their hands farther, as a result of all the practice they get from playing chords or octaves, and have an advantage in this game for 2 people.*

**PLAYING SURFACE:** ground or flat surface
**TECHNIQUE:** knuckles down

## Setup

1 Draw a shooting line.

## How to play

1 Player 1 rolls a marble any distance from the line. This is the target marble.

2 The second player tries to hit the target marble from behind the shooting line.

3 Any player who can hit a target marble or get within a handspan of it gets back her shooter.

4 Any player not within a handspan loses her marble to Player 1.

5 After each round, the players rotate. The last person to shoot rolls a target marble and all the other players shoot again. The game continues until all the players have had a turn rolling a marble.

### SCORING

The player who gets the most marbles wins.

# String of Beads

*This is a favorite of many players, and beginners find it easy to master. For 2 more more players.*

**PLAYING SURFACE:** smooth, flat surface, ground, pavement, or marble mat
**TECHNIQUE:** knuckles down

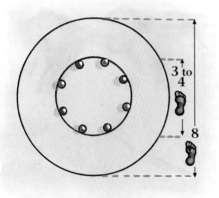

## Setup

1 Draw a circle about 3 to 4 feet (90 to 120 cm) in diameter, or use the 3- or 4-foot circle on the marble mat.

2 Draw a circle about 8 feet (240 cm) in diameter around the first circle. The 8-foot circle is the shooting line.

## How to play

1 Each player puts 4 to 5 marbles into the pot.

2 Place the marbles around the inner circle, leaving a space between the marbles (see diagram). This is the "string of beads."

3 Players take turns shooting a marble at the target marbles from outside of the large circle. If a player knocks a target marble off the string, it belongs to him. He must remove it and continue

playing until he misses or shoots his marble out of the ring.

**4** A player should not move his shooter after it stops rolling. The player takes his next shot from wherever it ends up.

### SCORING

**1** A marble knocked out counts as one point for the player who knocked it out.

**2** If you miss a target marble on your turn, you have to add a marble to the string of beads.

**3** The winner is the player with the most marbles when all the marbles have been knocked from the string of beads.

# Tic-Tac-Toe

*You've probably played tic-tac-toe on paper,*
*but how about tic-tac-toe with marbles?*
*Here's a game for 2 players.*

**PLAYING SURFACE:** flat surface indoors or outdoors
**TECHNIQUE:** any method

## Setup

1 Each person needs about 5 marbles that are of a different color or design than the other person's.

2 Draw a tic-tac-toe square as large or as small as you wish. You can use a stick to trace the design on the ground, or chalk for a sidewalk or on a cloth indoors.

3 Draw a shooting line 10 feet (3 m) away from an edge of the square.

4 Lag to see who goes first.

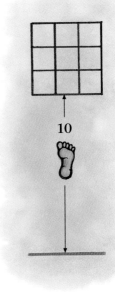

10

## How to play

1 Players stand behind the shooting line and take turns trying to make a line of three marbles by shooting marbles into the squares. The line could be straight or diagonal.

2 It is permissible to knock your opponent's marble from the square it occupies.

3 If you miss a square, pick up your marble.

**4** If another marble already is in a square, you can't occupy it unless you knock the other marble out.

## SCORING

The winner is the first person to get 3 marbles in a straight or diagonal line. At the end of the game, players get back their original marbles.

## STRATEGY

When it's played on paper, there is a way to win or tie every game of tic-tac-toe. Here's the secret. Label the squares as follows:

| A | B | C |
|---|---|---|
| D | E | F |
| G | H | I |

**1** If you go first, place your X in any corner (A, C, G, or I).

**2** Your opponent places an O anywhere else.

**3** For your next turn, place your X in another corner.

**4** Your opponent now has to place an O between your Xs.

Depending on your opponent's first move, you can now do one of two things:

**1** Place your X to stop the opponent getting 3 in a row.

**2** Place your X in a third corner. When this happens, you win every time.

# MARBLE
# ARCADES

There's more to marbles than just hitting other marbles! You can create you own arcade, using simple materials you find around your house. When the weather is too nasty to play outdoors, or when your parents have barred you from the TV, video game, or computer, here's a way to have fun and practice your marble skills all at the same time. You can play many of these games by yourself as well as with other players.

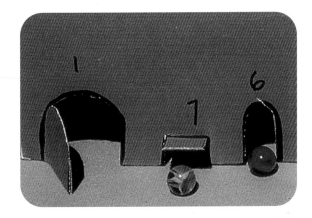

# Croquet

*In Alice in Wonderland, by Lewis Carroll, Alice played croquet using a flamingo as a mallet to hit the balls. A bird is not recommended as equipment in sports, but you can have fun using marbles. A game for 4 players.*

**PLAYING SURFACE:** smooth, flat surface
**TECHNIQUE:** any method

## You Will Need

- 3 or 4 white polystyrene or paper coffee cups
- scissors
- masking tape
- a marble for each player
- felt marker

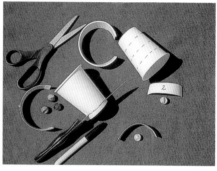

Supplies for Croquet. At lower right, a wicket on its side.

## Setup

1 Have an adult cut the base off a polystyrene or paper cup (see photo). This will give you a cylindrical shape. Cut the cylinder into 1-inch-wide (2.5 cm wide) rings; then cut each ring in half with scissors to form 2 semicircles. These are the gates (or wickets). Make a total of 9 gates the same way.

Wicket for Croquet.

2 Place the semicircles randomly around the area. Use masking tape to ensure that the semicircles stand in place. Number them from 1 to 9.

3 Draw a shooting line 1 foot (30 cm) in front of the first gate.

# How to play

**1** Lag to see who goes first.

**2** The first player starts anywhere on the shooting line and tries to shoot her marble through gate #1.

**3** If the marble goes through the gate, the player tries to shoot it through the next gate (gate #2).

**4** A player may hit another player's marble far off the playing field. The player who does this will not lose a turn. The player who has knocked the opponent's marble off out of play returns her own marble to the place it first came in contact with the other player's marble and takes the next shot from this spot.

**5** A player keeps shooting at the gates in numbered order until she misses a gate. If she misses, the next player shoots.

### SCORING
The first player to successfully get her target marble through all the gates wins. No marbles are exchanged, unless previously agreed before the game.

### VARIATION
You can also play Croquet following the same rules and game setup as is used in real croquet, but shooting a single marble through the gates with your fingers instead of using a ball and a mallet.

# Obstacles

## or Black Snake

*In most obstacle courses, the idea is to avoid the objects.*
*In this game, you have to hit the obstacles.*
*For 2 or more players.*

**PLAYING SURFACE:** smooth or flat surface
**TECHNIQUE:** any method

## You Will Need

- 7 different objects: for example, shoes, books, rocks, bottles
- marbles

Supplies for Obstacles.

## How to play

1 Place the items randomly around the playing area. Agree on the order in which you have to hit them, or label the objects 1 through 7.

2 Lag to see who goes first.

3 Move 1 foot away from the first object and shoot at it. If you hit it, you get another turn. You can move a handspan way from the object you just hit, and then shoot your marble towards the next object. You must hit each object in order. Keep shooting until you miss an object. Then it's the next person's turn.

**4** If you hit all the obstacles once and then go through from 1 to 7 again, you become a "black snake" and may take your marble and begin shooting other people's marbles off the course.

**5** There can be more than one black snake. If a black snake hits another person's shooter, that person is out of the game. However, if a black snake shoots another player's marble into an object, the snake is out of the game.

**PENALTY**
If you hit an obstacle out of order, you must start again.

**SCORING**
The last player to remain in the game wins.

# Bridges

## or Archboard

*This game uses a combination of marble skill and betting.*
*You are betting that your opponent can't get a marble into a slot and*
*your opponent is betting a marble that the shot can be made.*
*For 2 or more players.*

**PLAYING SURFACE:** smooth, flat surface
**TECHNIQUE:** knuckles down

## You Will Need

- old shoebox
- scissors
- felt markers
- marbles
- shoe or other heavy object

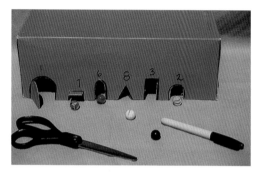

Finished box for Bridges.

## What to Do

1 Cut several holes of different widths in the long side of a shoebox. Each hole should be wide enough for a marble to go through.

2 Write any number from 1 to 10 above each hole. Tip: Give a small number to the widest hole and a large number to the smallest hole.

3 Place a shoe or other heavy object on top of the box to keep it from moving when hit by a marble.

4 Move an agreed-upon distance away from the box. Draw a line from which all players must shoot.

# GAME 1

**1** Take turns shooting at the holes. You have only one chance per turn to get your marble through the opening.

**2** If the player misses, his marble gets left where it is.

**3** If the marble goes through the hole, the player collects the marked number of marbles from the playing area. Example: you shoot your marble through the hole marked 3; you collect 3 marbles.

# GAME 2

**1** Take turns shooting. If a player gets the marble through a hole, the other players pay him the same number of marbles as is indicated on the hole.

**2** If the player misses, an opponent keeps the marble.

# GAME 3

**1** Agree among the players on the number of shots each person can take. Each player gives an agreed-to number of marbles into the pot.

**2** Take turns shooting at the holes. Keep score for each time you get through a hole.

**3** At the end of the game, add up the scores made by each person. The player with the most points wins the pot.

# INDEX